Nellie Bly: First Woman of the News

by
Tom Lisker

Illustrated by
Jeffrey Lindberg

cpi
contemporary perspectives, inc.

This book is distributed by Silver Burdett Company, Morristown, New
Jersey, 07960.

Library of Congress Number: 78-14382

Art and Photo Credits

Cover illustration by Jeffrey Lindberg
Photos on pages 27 and 29, Photoworld
Photo on page 41, The Granger Collection
Photo on page 47, Culver Pictures, Inc.
Every effort has been made to trace the ownership of all copyrighted
material in this book and to obtain permission for its use.

Library of Congress Cataloging in Publication Data

Lisker, Tom, 1928-
  Nellie Bly: First Woman of the News

  SUMMARY: A biography of one of the first women reporters, whose
trip around the world in less than eighty days made her an
international celebrity.
  1. Cochrane, Elizabeth, 1867-1922 — Biography — Juvenile
literature. 2. Journalists — United States — Biography — Juvenile
literature. [1. Cochrane, Elizabeth, 1867-1922. 2. Journalists]

I. Title.
PN4874.C59L5   070′.92′4   [B] [92] 78-14382
ISBN 0-89547-057-8

Manufactured in the United States of America
ISBN 0-89547-057-8

Contents

Chapter 1

Get Me Out of Here!

The nurse led Nellie Bly into a big room. There was a high ceiling and bars covered all the windows. There must have been 75 women in the room. All were dressed in shapeless gray gowns. The room and the people in it were like nothing Nellie had ever seen or dreamed about. Many of the women were talking — even screaming — to themselves. Nellie heard someone saying, over and over, "It wasn't me . . . it wasn't me!" The words came from an old woman standing near her. Another woman, seated on a low bench, was moving her hands as if she was sewing. She held neither thread nor needle. Still she kept on sewing . . . sewing . . .

Everything about the room was dirty. The windows were so covered with dust they let in little light. As her eyes got used to the dark, Nellie could make out the long rows of women chained to one another.

Nellie had never backed down from a story before. But she wasn't sure she could go through with this one. Still it could be the story of the century. If she ever got out to write it.

"Here's another one. She's not sure what her name is. She thinks it's Nellie," said the nurse who had brought her from the clothing room to this horrible place. Nellie tried to stay calm, but her fear was growing by the second. *Can I possibly stay here for a whole week?*

The nurse turned and left. The heavy, iron doors clanged shut. Nellie Bly — reporter for the *New York World* — was now on her own. The world's first woman reporter was locked away on Blackwell's Island — an asylum for the insane. No one there, besides herself, knew she was only there to write a story.

"Bath time!" yelled a nurse. The women ran to hide in the corners of the room. "Get over here or I'll send the whole rotten bunch of you to The Lodge." Some of the older women screamed in fear. They moved into line right away.

They are terrified of The Lodge, Nellie thought. During the week she was going to be there, she

Nellie was given a rough scrubbing.

figured she had better stay out of The Lodge —
whatever that was.

"O.K., you, in you go." Two nurses lifted Nellie off
her feet. They dropped her in the same cold bathwater
five other women had used. She was given a rough
scrubbing by a nurse.

"I can bathe myself," said Nellie.

"Shut up!" she was told.

The nurses lifted her from the tub. They gave her
the same towel that had been used to dry the other
women. Nellie didn't want to use the towel. Most of
these women had lice. "You do what you're told, or it'll
be The Lodge for a few days!" Nellie kept the dirty
towel.

The days were long on Blackwell's Island. Nellie had
time to make a few friends. She learned of several
women who had been sent there by mistake. Luckily

some of them were able to hold their minds together. Nellie could not imagine how they did. A week crawled by. Then it was eight days . . . nine. There was hardly enough food to keep a person alive. The food they served was almost too awful to eat. A new fear was growing in Nellie's mind. Had her boss at the newspaper forgotten all about her? Could that be? *Might she have to spend the rest of her life in this place?*

By the end of the ninth day, Nellie pleaded with the doctors to let her out. "I know my name," she told them. "I tell you I *do* know it! I'm Nellie Bly. I'm a newspaper reporter, with the *World* — the only woman reporter in New York." She was wasting her breath. The doctors ignored her.

Something had gone wrong. Nellie knew that — after nine days. But what? *Mr. Pulitzer promised to get me out in one week. What's wrong?*

To make the time pass, she thought back over the last few years. How had she wound up in this place? And so soon after coming to New York. If it were not so sad, it might even be funny. Elizabeth Cochrane of Pittsburgh had just become the world's first woman reporter. What was her reward? She was living in an insane asylum!

Chapter 2

What Girls Are Good For

It was November 1885. The small, slim 17-year-old girl stood in front of the gray building reading the stone letters on the cold, gray wall — the *Pittsburgh Dispatch*. She took a deep breath. It was the kind you take at the end of a diving board, just before you jump. Then she walked into the office building, up the stairs, and through the big, heavy door.

Inside were row upon row of men sitting at desks. Only men — everywhere she looked. Suddenly the noise of the busy city newsroom came to a stop. Only the rumble of the presses in the basement below went on. And if the men running the presses had been able to see what was happening two floors above them, they

A woman in a newspaper office was a strange sight in 1885.

would have stopped too. *A woman had actually entered the newspaper office!*

The young girl walked straight through some swinging doors. She looked neither right nor left. She was headed for the office marked, George A. Madden — Editor. A man who sat at one of the many desks gave a long whistle in amazement.

The girl gave a quick look back at the men who were silently watching her every move. Then she opened the door and walked in. The door closed firmly behind her.

The man behind the cluttered desk didn't even look up. Was he in for a surprise! "Well — what is it?" Madden barked between bites on his cigar.

Elizabeth Cochrane stood firmly in front of the desk. Her feet were slightly spread apart. Only her hands showed how nervous she was. They were holding onto her pocketbook for dear life. Her long, dark coat reached the floor and hid her black high-button shoes. She stared at the man behind the desk and said nothing. She waited. She had never been so scared in her life. After a moment, Mr. Madden raised his eyes to meet Elizabeth's. He was so surprised he almost swallowed his cigar. "What are you doing here, young lady? This is a newspaper office!"

12

The desk nameplate reads: GEORGE A. MADDEN

"I'm aware of that, Mr. Madden, but if you remember, we have an appointment," Elizabeth replied.

"I have no appointment with any young lady. And if you'll excuse me, I'm very busy right now. I will see you to the door." Mr. Madden started to get up.

"Just a moment, sir." Elizabeth seemed to lift her head an inch or two higher. "I am Elizabeth Cochrane. I see you have read my note. It's right there on your desk."

Elizabeth reached over and picked up a piece of paper lying on Mr. Madden's desk. She read it aloud:

"Mr. George A. Madden
Editor
Pittsburgh Dispatch
Pittsburgh, Pennsylvania

Dear Sir:
In reply to your request, I am the writer who answered your editorial 'What Girls Are Good For.' May I suggest next Wednesday afternoon at three o'clock for our appointment? If I do not hear from you to the contrary, I will be at your office at that time.

Sincerely, E. Cochrane"

"But you didn't say you were a woman! How was I supposed to know E. Cochrane was *Elizabeth* Cochrane?"

"Your note in the paper offered the writer a job. Well, I'm the writer," Elizabeth said firmly.

George Madden didn't answer. He just sat back in his chair and looked at the young girl for a second or two. Then he spoke. "O.K. I don't have all day. What's on your mind. You know I can't hire a woman as a reporter. Newspaper work is man's work."

"May I sit down?" Elizabeth asked sweetly.

"Oh ... oh — why, yes, of course," stammered Madden, remembering his manners. Elizabeth sat on the edge of a brown leather chair. She kept looking right at the editor. And she kept smiling.

"Your foolish editorial said that girls belong in the home," she reminded him. "It said how terrible it was that some girls were actually going out to get jobs. They would be taking jobs from men. The next thing you know they'll be wanting to vote. And if women are ever allowed to do that, the country will never be the same."

"I remember what I wrote, Miss Cochrane."

"Well, perhaps you also remember what I wrote. Men are not the only people in America with brains and ability. Women can do much more than marry, have children, cook, and clean house. In fact, the way women are treated is robbing this country of more than half the brains and skills of its citizens! I believe that, Mr. Madden. I believe that from the bottom of my heart. Don't *you*? You must! Otherwise, why did you ask me to come here?"

"Miss Cochrane, I *did not* ask you to come here!"

"You most certainly *did.*" Elizabeth reached into her pocketbook and took out a clipping. This was in your very own newspaper just last week.

"Will the gentleman who wrote a letter to the *Pittsburgh Dispatch,* criticizing our editorial of Friday, entitled 'What Girls Are Good For,' please send his name and address to the editor? Mr. Madden would like to talk with you about writing a feature article on the same subject for this paper."

Elizabeth put down the clipping. "Mr. Madden, *I am that gentleman.*" She stopped talking for a moment. Then she said, "Look, you can use a good reporter. And I need a job. You seem like a very smart man. Sending me away doesn't seem very smart. Does it?"

Mr. Madden said nothing for what seemed like hours to Elizabeth. She wondered if he knew how hard her heart was pounding. At last he rose slowly to his feet and smiled. "Miss Cochrane," he said, "I must be crazy, but you're hired."

"Oh, Mr. Madden!" Elizabeth heard herself scream with delight. "You won't be sorry. I'll work so hard you'll — " She didn't even finish the sentence. Tears of happiness came to her eyes. She had thought her dream might never come true. But it was coming true this very moment!

"However, you can't come to the office. Women are not allowed in the city room and I hope they never will be! Do you understand? Now, here's your first job. I want you to write a feature on 'Divorce' and send it in to me by the end of the week."

Elizabeth Cochrane walked out of the office like a proper young lady. But once she passed through the doors, she danced down the front steps of the *Dispatch*. She had a job! She was going to be a newspaper writer. She wasn't even aware that she had just made history!

Chapter 3

A New Job — A New Name

Elizabeth reached the street, and her dancing heart suddenly seemed to stop. "What do I know about divorce?" she asked herself. "Nothing. Well, you're going to have to learn something about it — and fast."

Elizabeth's father had been a judge before he died. He was the kind of man who made his daughter take things into her own hands and get them done. When she asked questions, he didn't just give her answers. He told her where to find the answers. Everything she learned from her father would come in handy on her first writing job. And there was one other thing about her father that might help.

Judge Cochrane had handled many divorce cases. She looked through his notes and added her own ideas.

She felt strongly that people should have the right to get divorced and live apart if they find themselves in a bad marriage. That was not a popular idea in the late 1800s. Elizabeth was far ahead of her time in many ways.

Her newspaper story was bright and well-written. She mailed it to the *Dispatch*, and Mr. Madden decided to print it. He wrote Elizabeth a note, telling her it would run in Sunday's *Dispatch*. He also told her to get started on a story about Grubacher's — a factory in Pittsburgh's slum area.

Elizabeth couldn't wait for the week to end. When Sunday came, she couldn't wait until the *Dispatch* was delivered. And then she couldn't wait until after church. In the Cochrane family you never looked at the newspaper before church.

Finally, after dinner, Elizabeth's mother, uncle, and six brothers began reading the paper. Elizabeth waited to see how surprised everybody would be. She had not told anybody in the family about her new job. But if they had come across her story so far, they did not talk about it. Everybody sat and read the paper. No one said a word.

Could it be that the story had not been run after all? Elizabeth couldn't wait any longer. She looked quickly through the paper. Sure enough, there it was. Her article! The big headline read, "Divorce." But the name under it was not hers at all. The name of the writer was *Nellie Bly*.

When Mr. Madden read Elizabeth's story he had an idea. The writing was good. But how would it look to have a young woman from a fine family like the Cochranes working on a newspaper? So he chose the name Nellie Bly, from a popular Stephen Foster song called "Nelly Bly." He just spelled it a little differently.

Elizabeth stood in the middle of the living room. "I have something to tell you," she said. "It's something wonderful!" Her big, brown eyes sparkled with pride and excitement. Everybody in the family thought for sure she was going to say she was getting married. After all, they felt a girl of Elizabeth's age should be thinking of marriage. But that's not what her family heard.

"I have a job with the *Dispatch*. I am a reporter. And look, everybody, here is my first feature story. I am Nellie Bly!"

"You're what?" her oldest brother asked. He didn't seem happy as he got up to take another look at the story in the paper.

"Oh, Elizabeth!" gasped her mother, quite ready to cry in shame.

Elizabeth waited as her family read the newspaper.
But no one said anything.

"The next thing you know, they'll send you into saloons!" said her uncle. He threw down the newspaper as if he wanted all of this to go away.

Everyone talked at once. They had all kinds of advice for Elizabeth. They told her to be a teacher or a nurse, if she wanted to work at all before she got married. But she should definitely not become a newspaper woman. It just wasn't done.

"I know you're all thinking of me and not yourselves," said Elizabeth with a smile. "But I can decide for myself. My mind is made up. I also think our father would have been proud of me."

That was the right thing to say. Suddenly Elizabeth's mother got up and hugged her warmly. "You're right! He certainly would have, my little Elizabeth. Or do we call you Nellie now? I, for one, am very proud of you. Your uncle and brothers will be proud of you too. They just have to come to their senses."

Sadly the men never did "come to their senses." But they couldn't stop Nellie Bly. She was a reporter. The story she had to write would not wait for the times to catch up with her ideas.

Chapter 4

Stop Nellie Bly

Could anyone really ask people to work in a place like this?

Nellie Bly asked herself how any human being could work, day after day, in the Grubacher factory. One look around this room told her why she was sent. The *Dispatch* wanted to tell the world what life was like for people who worked in factories like this one. "So this is a *sweatshop*," Nellie thought to herself.

The big room was cold, damp, and poorly lit. Water dripped down dirty walls. Long rows of women worked at the endless tables. Poorly dressed for the cold, workers bent over machines. Most wore rags wrapped around their feet to keep a little warmer. No one spoke. There was no use in trying to be heard over the roar of the machines.

A pocket watch factory at the end of the 19th century. The women are seated so that they can't talk to each other.

A rat scurried past Nellie and ran under one of the big machines. She saw another in a corner, eating a piece of bread. Not one worker seemed to even see.

Nellie walked upstairs. A photographer from the *Dispatch* was taking a picture of the manager in his bright, clean office. But Nellie Bly wanted to know what it was really like to work in the Grubacher factory. She did not think she would find out from the manager. She walked back into the nightmare on the floor below.

The working women talked openly to Nellie about their jobs. Long hours on their feet ... poor pay ... cold and damp ... one small bathroom for all the men and women who worked on two factory floors. These were the kinds of notes Nellie wrote as she talked with workers. Her story would really be her own feelings about the lives of these workers.

When the story ran in the *Dispatch*, the newspaper sold out. People ran around the city trying to buy copies. Of course, there was anger over Nellie Bly's story of the Grubacher sweatshop. The owner thought he would find pictures of himself and his office. But the pictures in the story showed workers who had to wrap their feet in rags because of the cold. Nellie's words were a sharp attack on owners who made people work in such places as Grubacher's.

The owners struck back. They wrote to important people all over the city. They spoke to church groups. "Who is this Nellie Bly?" they asked. "How dare a *woman* mix into things that are not her business. She is no lady, she is immoral!"

But Nellie Bly was now the voice of the working people. They wanted more stories from this woman. So did George Madden and the *Pittsburgh Dispatch*. Nellie was selling more newspapers than they had ever sold before.

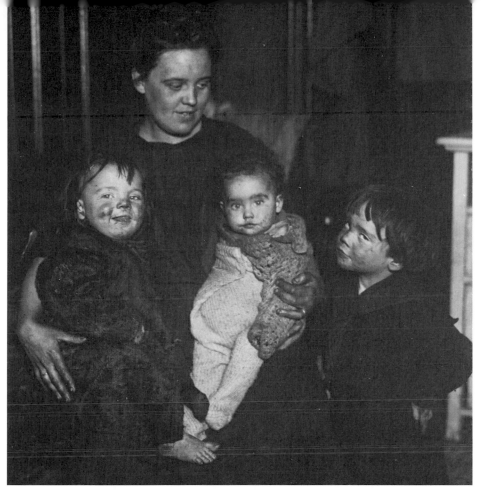

Life was not happy for the families of poor working people around the turn of the century.

So Nellie gave her boss and readers more of what they wanted. She went into the slums, and she told Pittsburgh what was happening to its poor men, women, and young people. Children of 10 and 12 were working long hours in the mills. The few extra pennies they earned kept their families from starving. She wrote about people who lived in dirty, unsafe slum houses. And about people who lived with disease and death always around the corner.

"These are our people," wrote Nellie. "Our brothers and sisters who are entitled to life and education and happiness as much as we are. Look at what we are doing to them!"

Nellie Bly became the eyes of the city. She took her readers into streets and homes where they would never dare to go on their own. Day after day, people snapped up the *Dispatch*. They all wanted to go where Nellie took them. They all wanted to know what she had to say. And week after week, there were more important people trying to stop George Madden and the *Dispatch* from telling Nellie's stories. "Stop Nellie Bly or lose our advertising money," some landlords and businessmen were saying. And, in time, they won. The paper could not do without their advertising.

So Nellie was given a new job. She became the music and drama critic. The owners of the *Dispatch* breathed a lot easier. The Cochrane family felt better too. Music and dance seemed more like a woman's work. Those stories about life in the slums were not for women to write. They were so . . . *dirty!*

The only person who was not happy with Nellie's new job was Nellie herself. She begged Mr. Madden to let her write the kind of stories she loved and did so well. He wanted her to, he told her. Very much. But Nellie found that she was asked for very few of "her kind of stories" from then on.

Chapter 5

Good Stories Come From Real Life

"I know it's hard work, but I want the job," Nellie said to the big factory foreman. She wanted to do another story on life in a factory. This time she would live that life first.

The foreman stopped talking to Nellie long enough to yell down to a group of women working in the cellar.

"Hey, you don't get paid for no daydreamin' down there. You work! And if you don't like the work, you can get yourself right out of here." Then he showed Nellie what she had to do. Her job was to tie copper wires into knots, over and over again. He stood over her while she got her first lesson.

"You have to go faster than that, Sweetie. I want to see those lovely white hands get dirty, just like everybody else's."

Nellie forced her fingers to go as fast as they could. It wasn't long before the wires cut her skin. Trickles of blood started to run down her hands. Nellie looked at the women near her. She could see their hands were tough and hard. Their bodies hurt from bending over the tables. They had to strain to see in the poor light. Nellie kept on working. But now that the foreman had gone, she began to question the other women. She heard the same story she had heard in the past — dirt, long hours, low pay, no heat, and poor light. But now she was seeing all of it firsthand. She was answering many of her own questions.

After one day Nellie's hands had become very bloody. She got up from her workbench to wash them off in some cold water. As she went to the filthy sink she heard the foreman yell again. This time it was at her. "Get back to your bench, and don't waste time about it! Nobody does anything around here without asking me first."

Nellie had had it. "I don't have to ask anyone if I want to wash my hands!" She was fired. But she

32   Nellie's new boss watched as she learned to tie the wires togethe

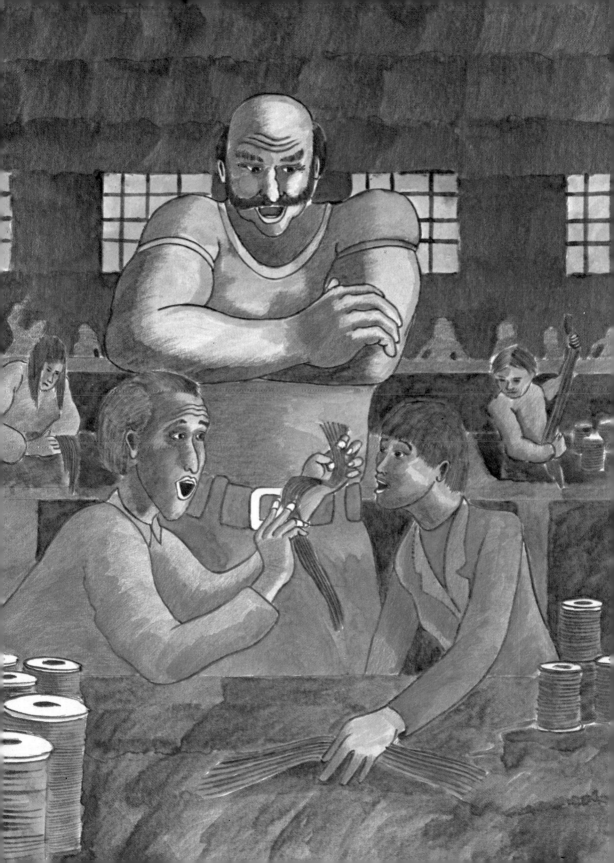

already had the story she was after. More importantly, it was the inside story.

It was the strongest writing Nellie had ever done. The *Dispatch* printed her story just as it was written. But it was the last such story they would print. Some rich and powerful people in the city had had enough. Either Nellie Bly stops writing stories like that *or else*. Mr. Madden gave Nellie a raise in salary to $15.00 a week. Then he put her back to writing about music, the theatre, and the arts.

It had now been more than a year since Nellie began to work as a reporter. Her stories about the theatre and the arts in and around Pittsburgh were very good. And they didn't bother anyone. It looked like Nellie had a nice, clean job for life. She was even invited to join the Pittsburgh Press Club. This was something that had never happened to another woman. Her family was, at last, proud of Nellie. As for Nellie, herself? She was not happy at all.

So one bright morning in 1887, Nellie walked into Mr. Madden's office to quit her job and say goodbye. She was going to New York. Nellie Bly was going to be a reporter for the *New York World*. At least that's the job she would try to get.

"I don't have to ask anyone if I want to want to wash my hands!" ▶

Chapter 6

A New York Reporter

It was summertime, 1887. Nellie felt as steaming hot as the city streets. She had stopped at a peanut stand on the way to the *World* offices. She had not had time for breakfast. A bag of peanuts would be lunch. But when Nellie reached for her pocketbook it was gone. She must have left it on the trolley car. Now she was alone in New York City, and she didn't have a cent to her name.

Here she was, waiting three hours to see the *World* editor, John Cockerill. She had sneaked by the guard who would not let her into the building. She had ducked out of sight every time someone walked by. Now she saw a man moving toward her from the steps. Well, she would not hide again. "Mr. Cockerill?" she asked in her sweetest voice. She was stunned when the man looked up and smiled. It was he!

In Mr. Cockerill's office, Nellie told him about her past work at the *Pittsburgh Dispatch*. Her former boss, Mr. Madden, had already written to the *World* about Nellie's good work. Mr. Cockerill told her he had no job open at the moment. But Nellie would not take no for an answer. She kept talking.

"I don't write *about* things. I *feel* them. I don't write *about* unhappy, unfortunate people. I *live* with them. I *work* with them. I *become* one of them. And that's why my stories are like nobody else's. Mr. Cockerill, I have an idea. I've heard some horrible stories about the way people are treated in the asylum on Blackwell's Island. If you hire me, I'll get myself sent there, and —"

Nellie had not heard the footsteps behind her. She didn't know that a man had entered Cockerill's office. He stood there behind her, listening. Suddenly he spoke.

"And how do you suppose you'll make the doctors think you're insane?"

Nellie turned to face Joseph Pulitzer, owner of the *World*. She had seen his picture. This was her chance. She felt small and unimportant in front of this famous man. But that didn't stop Nellie.

"I can get on Blackwell's Island. I just know I can. The only thing is, you'll have to get me off."

38

The two men looked at each other and nodded in agreement.

"O.K., Nellie Bly," said Mr. Pulitzer. "Go down to the cashier." He wrote something on a piece of paper and signed it. "Give him this. He'll give you some money. Next you must get yourself sent to the Blackwell's Island asylum. We will give you one week there, and then our lawyers will get you out. But Nellie, your story had better be a *knockout*."

Now Nellie was remembering Mr. Pulitzer's last words to her.

She sat in her shapeless gray gown. With her bare feet and her loose, stringy hair she looked like all the others on Blackwell's Island. "Only one difference," she thought. "I am here to get a story, and I should have been out of here three days ago. Well, Mr. Pulitzer, my story is a 'knockout.' But will anyone ever read it?"

Getting to the island had been almost as hard as it now seemed to be to get off. She had moved to a hotel for women. Her name, she said, was hard to remember. She did everything she could to make everyone think she was out of her mind. She would

Nellie Bly had a hard time getting to Blackwell's Island, but she made it.

scream and cry in the night. She would run around yelling, "They're after me. Get my gun!" After a few nights of this the hotel manager called the police. Nellie's plan was starting to work.

A judge had five doctors look at Nellie. They watched her for a few days. Nellie acted in the strangest ways she could dream up. The doctors finally told the judge she was hopeless. The only safe place for Nellie would be Blackwell's Island. And the sooner she got there, the better. Now Nellie had been on Blackwell's Island for ten days. No one would listen to her when she told them she didn't belong there. "That's what they all say," she was told by the doctors and nurses.

Just before dinner, a nurse came up to Nellie. There was a visitor to see her. He said he was an attorney from the *New York World*. The nurse seemed puzzled that he should be visiting this place. But Nellie knew why he was here. "Freedom," she thought. While her heart sang, Nellie walked to the visitor's room with tears in her eyes. She was happy to be leaving, but what about all the others who had to stay?

The doctors told the judge
Nellie was a hopeless case.

Chapter 7

The Best Reporter in the U.S.

The *World* stories about Blackwell's Island hit New York like a clap of thunder. Nellie Bly's ten-day stay shocked the city and the nation. People pressed the city government for action — more money for mental hospitals, more doctors and nurses, and cleaner housing. Nellie's stories were selling newspapers. She was the most talked-about reporter in the country. But her happiest moment came when several of her new friends were found quite sane and left Blackwell's Island to start new lives.

For the next few years Nellie Bly seemed to be everywhere there was a story to be told. Mr. Pulitzer, John Cockerill, and the millions of *World* readers thrilled to every word she wrote. Once she became a dancer in a chorus line and did a story on stagestruck

Nellie even took a job as a dancer to get a story.

girls who come to New York City. Another time she pretended to be a rich woman who needed help from an important man in government. She offered to pay him a great deal of money in return for special help for her business. She then wrote a story that sent the man and many of his dishonest friends to jail.

The walls that had kept women from reporting the news were crumbling quickly. By 1895 women were working as reporters for a few magazines and newspapers all around the country. As for Nellie Bly, she had been around the world in a race with another woman reporter. A book by Jules Verne, *Around the World in Eighty Days*, was sweeping the country. Nellie wanted to make the trip in less than 80 days. Although Nellie didn't know it, another reporter was sent by a magazine to beat her. Mr. Pulitzer was not at all surprised to learn that Nellie had beaten both — the 80-day mark and the other reporter.

Nellie was a national idol after her race "round the world in 72 days." She wrote a best-selling book about the trip. The Pennsylvania Railroad called their fastest train "The Nellie Bly." A racehorse was named after her. There were Nellie Bly caps, coats, and dresses. There were songs written about her.

While covering a story in Chicago, Nellie met and married a man named Robert Seaman in 1895. After Seamen died in 1910, Nellie took over his business.

Elizabeth Cochrane — the famous "Nellie Bly."

But she soon returned to her first love — newspaper writing. She died on January 27, 1922.

A story in the August 1891 *Cosmopolitan* magazine tells us that a Mrs. J.C. Crody was really the first woman to work for a daily newspaper. She wrote under the name of "Jennie June." Perhaps that is true. But after reading the news stories covered by both women, Nellie Bly must still be called the first woman *reporter* to pave the way for future newspaper women. Whether she was first or second, Nellie probably would not have cared. What she would have been most proud of was what the *New York Journal* printed after her death: " . . . she was considered the best reporter in America."

A Final Word

When Nellie Bly died in 1922, she was almost penniless. Her grave was not even marked with a tombstone. In 1978 the New York Press Club gave Nellie Bly her final well earned honor. They put up a stone over her grave at Woodlawn Cemetery in New York City.